# Diet recommendations for TCM - Liver - Blood deficiency

Please check these recommendations always with a TCM nutrition consultant, therapist, doctor or dietician. The recipes and the list of ingredients are supporting also the conventional medical therapy. The calorie disclosures of fresh ingredients (fruit and vegetables) vary according to quality and time of harvest. The contents were checked by a dietician and a nutrition consultant for the Traditional Chinese Medicine (TCM).

Author:
©2017 Josef Miligui
www.ebns.at

AF285337

Source:
The lists are created from the EBNS database for nutritional counseling. The database is used by dietitians, therapists and doctors for advising the patient / client.

Literature:
The specialist literature and the training documents of the German and Austrian dietary and traditional Chinese medicine serve as a knowledge base. We have used the documents as a basis of knowledge, adapted it to our experience and completed them.
http://di-book.com

Title Photo:
©2008 Erika Weixlbaumer

Production and publishing:
BoD – Books on Demand, Norderstedt
ISBN: 9783752861365

# Diet recommendations for TCM - Liver - Blood deficiency

| | | |
|---|---|---|
| 1 | Treatment strategy | 3 |
| 2 | Avoid | 3 |
| 3 | Breakfast | 4 |
| 4 | Lunch | 4 |
| 5 | Dinner | 4 |
| 6 | Any time | 5 |
| 7 | Recipes | 6 |
| 7.1 | 8 treasures of rice | 6 |
| 7.2 | Barley soup | 6 |
| 7.3 | Basic recipe for a beef broth (clear) | 7 |
| 7.4 | Basic recipe for a chicken broth worming | 8 |
| 7.5 | Basic recipe for a duck broth | 8 |
| 7.6 | Basic recipe for a fish broth | 9 |
| 7.7 | Basic recipe for a reissue soup (Congee) | 10 |
| 7.8 | Basic recipe for a vegetable soup, nutritious | 10 |
| 7.9 | Beetroot soup with sauerkraut potato biscuits | 11 |
| 7.10 | Chicken soup with angelica root and buckthorn fruit | 12 |
| 7.11 | Chicken soup with egg yolk and parsley | 12 |
| 7.12 | Clear oxen tail soup with buckthorn fruit | 13 |
| 7.13 | Fruit soup with cherries, logane and lycii | 13 |
| 7.14 | Millet with egg and butter | 14 |
| 7.15 | Pumpkin curry | 15 |
| 7.16 | Red berry with beaters | 16 |
| 7.17 | Red grape juice with egg yolk | 16 |
| 7.18 | Red wine with egg yolk | 17 |
| 7.19 | Reissue soup with duck | 17 |
| 7.20 | Rice congee with chicken liver and buckthorn fruit | 18 |
| 7.21 | Rice with parsnips | 18 |
| 7.22 | Roasted millet with Celery sticks | 19 |
| 7.23 | Roasted nuts | 19 |
| 7.24 | Spinach with Tahini | 20 |
| 7.25 | Tea from coriander | 20 |
| 7.26 | Tea from Fructus Lycii | 20 |
| 7.27 | Tea from lemon | 21 |
| 7.28 | Tea from licorice (heart-strengthening) | 21 |
| 7.29 | Tea from longane | 22 |
| 7.30 | Tea from rose hip | 22 |
| 7.31 | Tea from rosemary | 22 |
| 7.32 | Tsampa with jam or fruit compote | 23 |

8    Effects of food.............................................................24
    8.1     Use ingredients: recommendable .........................24
    8.2     Use ingredients: yes.............................................28
    8.3     Use ingredients: little..........................................29
    8.4     Do not use contra-acting foods............................30
9    Herbs and their effects..............................................32
    9.1     Basil.....................................................................32
    9.2     Coriander..............................................................32
    9.3     Herbs various.......................................................32
    9.4     Cress....................................................................32
    9.5     Lily bulbs..............................................................32
    9.6     Marjoram..............................................................33
    9.7     Parsley..................................................................33
    9.8     Rosemary..............................................................33
    9.9     Sage......................................................................33
    9.10    King Solomon's-seal.............................................34
    9.11    Yam root, yam root tuber.....................................34
    9.12    Lemon Balm (fresh).............................................34
10   Basics of Nutrition......................................................35
    10.1    Nutrition................................................................35
    10.2    Recipes.................................................................37
    10.3    Foodstuffs............................................................37
    10.4    Herbs....................................................................38
11   Other dietic-books......................................................39

# 1    Treatment strategy

Nourish blood, strengthen middle and kidneys qi, harmonize liver.
Hot - NO, cold - NO, sour - LITTLE, warm - LITTLE (bitter NO, sweet
YES), neutral and refreshing YES

# 2    Avoid

Red wine, alcohol, black tea, green tea, yogic tea, mineral water, grilled,
smoked, fried, spicy hot spices, too much salt, tropical fruits, sugar,
marine fish except calamari, carp, cigarettes.

# 3  Breakfast

kkal. per serving

Barley soup.................................................................... 265
Fruit soup with cherries, logane and lycii ..................... 189
Millet with egg and butter ............................................ 338
Red berry with beaters................................................. 123
Red wine with egg yolk................................................. 242
Reissue soup with duck................................................ 160
Rice with parsnips........................................................ 206
Roasted millet with Celery sticks ................................ 400
Roasted nuts............................................................... 973
Tsampa with jam or fruit compote................................ 280

# 4  Lunch

8 treasures of rice ....................................................... 212
Barley soup.................................................................. 265
Beetroot soup with sauerkraut potato biscuits.............. 128
Chicken soup with angelica root and buckthorn fruit ...... 77
Chicken soup with egg yolk and parsley ....................... 117
Clear oxen tail soup with buckthorn fruit ...................... 217
Fruit soup with cherries, logane and lycii ..................... 189
Millet with egg and butter ............................................ 338
Pumpkin curry.............................................................. 193
Red berry with beaters ................................................ 123
Red wine with egg yolk................................................. 242
Reissue soup with duck................................................ 160
Rice congee with chicken liver and buckthorn fruit......... 175
Rice with parsnips........................................................ 206
Roasted millet with Celery sticks ................................ 400
Roasted nuts............................................................... 973
Spinach with Tahini ..................................................... 150

# 5  Dinner

Barley soup.................................................................. 265
Beetroot soup with sauerkraut potato biscuits.............. 128
Chicken soup with angelica root and buckthorn fruit ...... 77
Clear oxen tail soup with buckthorn fruit ...................... 217
Pumpkin curry.............................................................. 193
Red berry with beaters ................................................ 123
Red wine with egg yolk................................................. 242
Reissue soup with duck................................................ 160

Rice congee with chicken liver and buckthorn fruit.......................... 175
Rice with parsnips........................................................................ 206
Roasted millet with Celery sticks .................................................. 400
Roasted nuts............................................................................... 973
Spinach with Tahini .................................................................... 150

# 6   Any time

Red wine with egg yolk.................................................................. 242
Rice with parsnips........................................................................ 206
Roasted millet with Celery sticks .................................................. 400
Roasted nuts............................................................................... 973

# 7 Recipes

(recommendable) = You can use more.
(little) = You should use less than specified or omit.

## 7.1 8 treasures of rice

Strengthens kidney and bladder, builds up Qi, strengthens the spleen, repels moisture, reduces internal heat, prevents cancer, builds heart, calms nerves.
Cooking time approx. 1 hour
Calories p. portion: 212
4 portions

**Quantity of ingredients**
Lily bulbs  1 table spoon /  5g. (recommended)................................. *
Longane  1 table spoon /  5g. (yes) .................................................... *
King Solomon's-seal  1 table spoon /  5g. (recommended)................. *
Yam root, yam root tuber  1 table spoon /  5g. (recommended)........... *
Coix (seeds) YiYi Ren  1 table spoon /  5g. (yes)............................... *
Rice wild (nature rice)  1 1/2 cups /  240g. (yes) .......................... metal
Water  8-10 cups /  800g. (yes) .................................................. earth

**Cooking instructions:**
Each one 1 tbsp:  Bai He, Longan, Yu Zhu, Da Zao, Shan Yao, Lian Mi, Yi Yi Ren, Qian Shi
Add hot water and soak for about 30 minutes. Then add 1 - 2 cups of rice (normal) and simmer for 1/2 to 1 hour until the rice is very soft. Or: Cook for about 3 hours with the herbs a congee. Then the herbs do not have to be soaked.

## 7.2 Barley soup

Works neutral to slightly warming and relaxes the Qi flow. Helps with loss of appetite and diarrhea due to spleen weakness. With weak spleen qi, one should often eat salty soups for breakfast.
Cooking time approx. 25 min
Calories p. portion: 265
2 portions
Allergens: A

**Quantity of ingredients**

Barley  1 cup /  120g. (recommended)......................................... earth
Salt  1 pinch /  1g. (recommended)................................................water
Ginger fresh  1/2 teaspoon /  1g. (little).........................................metal
Olive oil  1 table spoon /  10g. (little)............................................. earth
Parsley  2 table spoons /  30g. (recommended)...........................wood
Water  1 1/2 cups /  240g. (yes).................................................... earth

**Cooking instructions:**

Roast the barley in the pan, then grind it to the ground, and boil with water, some salt and ginger to a mash. Before serving add oil and parsley.

Variant: You can add a better taste to the dish if you cook it with prepared vegetable or meat broth.


## 7.3    Basic recipe for a beef broth (clear)

Strengthens Qi and Yang, is very warming.
Cooking time approx. 4-8 hours
Calories p. portion: 114
10 portions
Allergens: O

**Quantity of ingredients**

Beef soup meat  1,1 lbs /  500g.  ................................................ earth
Beef meatbones  5/8 oz /  200g.  ................................................ earth
Vinegar (Red wine vinegar)  1 dash /  3g.  ..................................wood
Juniper berry  8 pieces /  6g.  ....................................................... fire
Rosemary  1 pinch /  1g.  .............................................................. fire
Carrot  3 pieces /  210g.  ............................................................ earth
Parsnip  2 pieces /  300g.  ............................................................ fire
Leek  1 piece /  200g.  .................................................................metal
Ginger fresh  1/2 teaspoon /  5g.  ...............................................metal
Lovage  1 stem /  15g.  ................................................................metal
Clove  2 pieces /  2g.  ..................................................................metal
Pimento  6 pieces /  12g.  ............................................................metal
Anise (Common Fennel)  2 pieces /  1g.  .................................... earth
Salt  1 teaspoon /  5g.  ................................................................water
Water  3,3 lbs /  1300g.  .............................................................. earth

**Cooking instructions:**
Heat water, a dash of red wine vinegar, some juniper berries, a little rosemary, bones and meat till it boils; add carrot, parsnip, leek, ginger, lovage, clove, allspice, star anise and a little salt; simmer for 4-8 hours then strain.
Refrigerate for later use.

## 7.4 Basic recipe for a chicken broth worming

Strengthens Qi and blood, is very warm.
Cooking time approx. 2-3 hours
Calories p. portion: 90
9 portions
Allergens: L

**Quantity of ingredients**
Chicken meat  1/2 piece /  600g.  ............................................... wood
Carrot  2 pieces /  150g.  .......................................................... earth
Leek  1 stick /  45g.  ..................................................................metal
Celery root  1 piece /  500g.  ...................................................... earth
Ginger fresh  2 slices /  2g. .......................................................metal
Fenugreek  (Trigonella foenum-graecum)  1 teaspoon /  2g.  .............*
Juniper berry  1 teaspoon /  3g.  .................................................... fire
Bay leaf  3 pieces /  2g.  ................................................................ *
Water  4 cup /  900g.  ................................................................ earth

**Cooking instructions:**
Remove chicken parts from fat. Place chicken pieces in a saucepan with hot water and heat till it boils briefly, skimming any resulting foam. Add coarsely chopped vegetables and all spices and cook over medium heat for 2 to 3 hours. Strain the finished soup. Throw away vegetables and bones.
Tip: If you want to use the meat as a soup insert, take out after 45 minutes and return only the bones in the soup.
Refrigerate for later use.

## 7.5 Basic recipe for a duck broth

Forces Qi, strengthens blood and fluids, nourishes Yin, forces stomach, cools heat, strengthens spleen and liver.
Cooking time approx. 2-3 hours
Calories p. portion: 61
6 portions
Allergens: L

## Quantity of ingredients

Duck (heart)  5/8 oz /  200g. ....................................................wood
Water  2 cup /  450g. ............................................................... earth
Duck (slaughtered)  1/4 lbs - 4oz /  100g. .................................wood
Carrot  2 pieces /  100g. .......................................................... earth
Celery root  1/2 piece /  600g. .................................................. earth

## Cooking instructions:

Cook duck pieces with vegetables for 2-3 hours. Sift broth through a fine sieve and refrigerate for later use.
The innards can be reused: You cut them finely and leaves them for a few minutes with fresh vegetables in the broth draw. Sprinkle with parsley before serving.

## 7.6   Basic recipe for a fish broth

Strengthens kidney Qi and Yin, strengthens blood and fluids, promotes urination.
Cooking time approx. 40 min
Calories p. portion: 128
5 portions
Allergens: DLO

## Quantity of ingredients

Fish pieces mixed (fresh water)  3/4 lbs /  300g. ........................water
Celery root  1/4 lbs - 4oz /  120g. ............................................. earth
Leek  2 inches /  10g. ............................................................metal
Carrot  2 pieces /  150g. .......................................................... earth
White wine  1/2 cup /  125g. ....................................................wood
Lemon  1/2 piece /  50g. ..........................................................wood
Bay leaf  2 leaves /  2g. ................................................................ *
Peppercorns  3 pieces /  2g. ....................................................metal
Olive oil  1 table spoon /  10g. .................................................. earth
Water  2 cup /  450g. ............................................................... earth

## Cooking instructions:

Fry celery, chopped carrots and leeks in olive oil, add bay leaf and peppercorns, add pieces of fish and sauté briefly. Add water, add little white wine or lemon. Simmer gently for 30 minutes. Skim off the resulting foam several times. In the end, sift the ingredients through a cloth. Refrigerate for later use.

## 7.7 Basic recipe for a reissue soup (Congee)

Warms the stomach and spleen, harmonizes the intestine, forces Qi,
reduces moisture.
Cooking time approx. 2-4 hours
Calories p. portion: 140
3 portions
Allergens:

### Quantity of ingredients
Rice variety any  1 cup /  120g.  ...............................................metal
Water  6 cups /  700g.  ............................................................ earth

### Cooking instructions:
Cook rice and water in a ratio of about 1: 6. The amount of water
determines the thickness of the mash (matter of taste).
Put the rice in a saucepan with a heavy lid. It is important to simmer the
rice after a short boil on the slightest flame, otherwise it burns.
Boil the rice for 2-4 hours. The longer he cooks, the more he
strengthens.
If you want to eat the dish for breakfast, you can put the rice on just
before bedtime.
To be on the safe side, you should first check the behavior of your pot
and cooker under observation for a similar amount of time, so that
nothing burns.
Refrigerate for later use.

## 7.8 Basic recipe for a vegetable soup, nutritious

Strengthens spleen and lung, regulates Qi flow, builds up Qi, dries out,
passes downwardly, strengthens stomach Qi.
Cooking time approx. 2-3 hours
Calories p. portion: 48
5 portions
Allergens: L

### Quantity of ingredients
Olive oil  1 table spoon /  4g.  ..................................................... earth
Onion white  1 piece /  60g.  ......................................................metal
Carrot  3 pieces /  200g.  ........................................................... earth
Parsnip  3/8 lbs - 6oz /  150g.  ...................................................... fire
Celery root  1 cup /  100g.  ......................................................... earth
Ginger fresh  1/2 teaspoon /  2g.  ...............................................metal
Lemon  1/2 piece /  25g.  ..........................................................wood

Juniper berry  6 pieces /  6g.  ....................................................... fire
Thyme dried  1 pinch /  1g.  ....................................................metal
Lovage  1 table spoon /  3g.  ..................................................metal
Bay leaf  2 leaves /  1g.  ...................................................................*
Salt  1 pinch /  1g.  ...............................................................water
Water  3 cups /  650g.  ........................................................... earth

## Cooking instructions:
Cut the vegetables into cubes.
Heat oil in hot pot, fry shortly onions and vegetables.
Add cold water, then add ginger, bay leaf and lemon juice.
Season with juniper, thyme and lovage. Cover for 2 - 3 hours on a low heat and simmer.
The used vegetables should be thrown away.
The basic recipe serves as a soup base and to refine vegetables, legumes or cereals.
If you want to eat vegetable soup immediately, add the desired vegetables half an hour before.
Refrigerate for later use.

## 7.9   Beetroot soup with sauerkraut potato biscuits

Strengthens spleen and liver, regulates Qi flow, relaxes, builds up Qi, spreads, strengthens stomach Qi.
Cooking time approx. 30 min
Calories p. portion: 128
2 portions
Allergens: GLN

### Quantity of ingredients
Red beet  1/4 lbs - 4oz /  125g. (recommended) .......................... earth
Potato  1 oz /  25g. (yes) ............................................................ earth
Basic recipe for a vegetable soup 1 cup /  250g. (recommended) .......*
Lemon juice  1/4 /  6g. (recommended) ...................................... wood
Salt  1 pinch /  0,5g. (recommended) ........................................... water
Sesame oil  1/2 teaspoon /  1g. (yes) ......................................... earth
Potato  1/8 lbs - 2oz /  50g. (yes) ............................................... earth
Butter organic  1 teaspoon /  10g. (yes) ..................................... earth
Sauerkraut (cutted cabbage fermented)  1 oz /  25g. (little) .......... wood
Cream sour 10%  1 teaspoon /  3g. (recommended) ...........................*
Sesame, white  1 teaspoon /  2g. (recommended) ...................... earth
Marjoram  1 pinch /  0,3g. (little) .................................................. metal
Salt  1 pinch /  0,5g. (recommended) ........................................... water

**Cooking instructions:**
Peel beetroot and potatoes and cut into small cubes, heat till it boils, add sesame oil and lemon juice and simmer for 20 minutes until the beetroot is tender.
For the cookies, the potatoes are peeled, cut into thin slices and buttered. Bake at 200°C/392°F in the oven for 1/4 hour until golden. Sweat finely chopped sauerkraut in butter, add sour cream, marjoram and salt. This mass is distributed on the potato slices, sprinkled with sesame seeds and baked for a few minutes at 200°C/392°F.
Puree the soup and season with salt and cream. Serve the finished soup with the sauerkraut and potato cookies.

## 7.10 Chicken soup with angelica root and buckthorn fruit

Strengthens spleen and nourishes the blood and Yin of the liver, forces Qi and blood, is very warming.
Cooking time approx. 1 1/2 hours
Calories p. portion: 77
3 portions
Allergens: LO

### Quantity of ingredients
Basic recipe for a chicken soup 2 cup / 500g. (recommended) .......... *
Angelica root  1/8 oz /  5g. (recommended) ...................................... *
Bocksdorn fruits, goji berry dried  1/8 lbs - 2oz /  50g. ................ wood

### Cooking instructions:
When you cook chicken broth according to basic recipes add angelica root and Bocksdorn fruits in the last 40 minutes.
Ingestion: Drink 2-3 cups of broth daily.

## 7.11 Chicken soup with egg yolk and parsley

Forces Qi and blood, is very warming, nourishes blood and liver, harmonizes liver and spleen, forces eyesight, preserves the fluids, contracts.
Cooking time approx. 10 min
Calories p. portion: 118
2 portions
Allergens: CL

**Quantity of ingredients**
Basic recipe for a chicken soup 2 cup / 500g. (recommended) ..........*
Chicken yolk  1 piece / 10g. (recommended) .............................. earth
Parsley  1 table spoon / 10g. (recommended)............................. wood

**Cooking instructions:**
Cook the chicken broth according to the basic recipe.
Heat broth and bubble the egg yolk. Sprinkle the chopped parsley over it and let it rest for about 2 minutes. Drink in small sips.

## 7.12 Clear oxen tail soup with buckthorn fruit

Forces  Qi, nourishes the liver blood, good for ocular fibrillation or dry eyes, muscle tension or calf cramps due to blood deficiency.
Cooking time approx. 1-2 hours
Calories p. portion: 217
6 portions
Allergens: O

**Quantity of ingredients**
Basic recipe for a beef soup 4 cup / 1000g. (recommended)..............*
Beef Oxtail pieces  1,1 lbs / 500g. (recommended) ..................... earth
Shiitake, dried  4-5 pieces / 4g. (yes).......................................... earth
Onion white  1 piece / 60g. (little)................................................ metal
Sake  2 table spoons / 20g. (recommended).............................. metal
Ginger fresh  1/2 teaspoon / 2g. (little).......................................... metal
Bocksdorn fruits, goji berry dried  1 table spoon / 8g. ................ wood

**Cooking instructions:**
Soak shiitake mushrooms. Blanch oxtail slices (This removes fat and impurities).
Cook in the beef broth for 1-2 hours.
Then add the spring onions, shiitake mushrooms, rice wine, buckthorn fruits and ginger and simmer gently.

## 7.13 Fruit soup with cherries, logane and lycii

Strengthens blood and fluids, regulates Qi, produces humors, calms the mind, forces Qi, supports skin regeneration, forces spleen, builds up lung, builds up heart, calms nerves, moisturizes liver and kidney, reduces internal heat.
Cooking time approx. 10 min
Calories p. portion: 190
2 portions

**Quantity of ingredients**

Cherry  1/4 lbs - 4oz /  100g. (recommended).............................. earth
Longane  1/4 lbs - 4oz /  100g. (yes) ......................................................... *
Lychee  1/4 lbs - 4oz /  100g. (recommended).................................... *
Lemon juice  2 cup /  10g. (recommended)................................. wood
Cherry juice  1/2 cup /  125g. (little) ............................................. wood
Sugar cane sugar  2 table spoons /  20g. () .............................. earth
Rice starch  1/8 oz /  5g. (recommended) ....................................metal
Water  1 cup /  250g. (yes)........................................................ earth
Acerola fruit nectar or powder  1 teaspoon /  2g. (rec.)................. wood

**Cooking instructions:**
Wash the cherries, drain and stone, peel and core the Lychee and
Logane. Boil water, sugar, fruits and lemon juice. Stir the starch until
smooth with water. Pour into the fruit with stirring, bring to the boil for 1
min and allow to cool. Stir in the acerola.

# 7.14 Millet with egg and butter

Forces blood, Yin and Jing, nourishes Yin, moisturizes in case of
internal dryness, forces blood, forces spleen, calms nerves and
stomach, strengthens spleen and kidney, diuretic, strengthens Qi and
kidney Jing, moisturizes, relaxes, builds up Qi, spreads.
Cooking time approx. 25 min
Calories p. portion: 338
2 portions
Allergens: CG

**Quantity of ingredients**

Millet  1 cup /  100g. (recommended).......................................... earth
Ginger fresh  1/2 teaspoon /  1g. (little).......................................metal
Salt  1 pinch /  0,5g. (recommended)...........................................water
Parsley  2 table spoons /  16g. (recommended)........................... wood
Pepper powder (hot)  1 pinch /  1g. (recommended) ...................... fire
Chicken egg  2 pieces /  100g. (little)........................................... earth
Butter organic  2 table spoons /  20g. (yes)................................. earth
Nutmeg  1 pinch /  0,2g. (little).....................................................metal
Water  1 1/2 cups /  200g. (yes)................................................... earth

**Cooking instructions:**
Simmer the millet with the ginger and nutmeg in the water for 5 min.
and let it swell for another 30 min.

Cook and peel 1 soft egg per person; pile up the millet on plates and place 1 egg each in a hollow in the millet mountain; Put butterflakes over it. Sprinkle with chopped parsley and the rose paprika.

## 7.15 Pumpkin curry

Forces lungs and spleen, diuretic, forces Qi, protects liver, warms the stomach and spleen, harmonizes the intestine, forces Qi, reduces moisture, moisturizes, relaxes, builds up Qi, spreads, nourishes blood and liver, harmonizes liver and spleen.
Cooking time approx. 20 min
Calories p. portion: 193
3 portions

### Quantity of ingredients
Pumpkin  3/4 lbs /  300g. (yes) .................................................... earth
Olive oil  2 table spoons /  30g. (little) .......................................... earth
Coriander  1 pinch /  1g. (recommended) .................................... metal
Pepper (ground)  1 pinch /  0,5g. () ............................................. metal
Curry  1 pinch /  1g. () ................................................................ metal
Water  1/4 cup /  50g. (yes) ......................................................... earth
Salt  1 pinch /  1g. (recommended) .............................................. water
Parsley  1 table spoon /  7g. (recommended) .............................. wood
Cardamom  1 pinch /  1g. (recommended) ............................................ *
Turmeric (yellow root)  1 pinch /  1g. (recommended) ......................... *
Rice (whole grain)  1/2 cup /  60g. (yes) ...................................... metal
Water  3 cups /  300g. (yes) ........................................................ earth
Salt  1 pinch /  1g. (recommended) .............................................. water

### Cooking instructions:
Heat olive oil in pan. Steam the pumpkin cut in cubes, season with cilantro, pepper and curry, simmer with a little water, salt with sea salt, add chopped parsley with cardamom and turmeric, simmer on a small fire for about 10 minutes, depending on the pumpkin, the pumpkin should still be firm.

Place the rice in salted water, bring to the boil and let it simmer over low heat for about 15 minutes.

## 7.16 Red berry with beaters

Builds up blood.
Cooking time approx. 15 min
Calories p. portion: 124
2 portions
Allergens: G

### Quantity of ingredients
Berries of the season  1 1/2 cups /  200g. (recommended) .......... wood
Grape juice red  1 cup /  200g. (recommended)........................... earth
Sugar molasses  1 table spoon /  10g. (yes)............................... earth
Vanilla  1 pinch /  0,2g. (yes) ................................................................. *
Cream (30% fat)  2 table spoons /  20g. (recommended).................... *

### Cooking instructions:
Put berries and red fruits (redcurrants, raspberries, strawberries, blackberries and blueberries) in a saucepan. Add half a glass of elderberry juice, half a glass of red wine or red grape juice. Add one tablespoon of sugarcane molasses and a pinch of vanilla. Simmer for a few minutes and serve with a bit of whipped cream.


## 7.17 Red grape juice with egg yolk

Tonifies Yin and Qi, brings blood into motion, exudes moisture, detoxifying, hematinic.
Cooking time approx. 5 min
Calories p. portion: 271
1 portions
Allergens: C

### Quantity of ingredients
Grape juice red  1 cup /  250g. (recommended)........................... earth
Chicken yolk  1 piece /  25g. (recommended) ............................. earth

### Cooking instructions:
Whisk egg yolks in grape juice.

## 7.18 Red wine with egg yolk

Dries out, passes downwardly.
Cooking time approx. 5 min
Calories p. portion: 242
1 portions
Allergens: CO

**Quantity of ingredients**
Red wine  1 cup /  200g. (recommended) ........................................ fire
Chicken yolk  1 piece /  25g. (recommended) .............................. earth

**Cooking instructions:**
Beat raw egg yolk in red wine.

## 7.19 Reissue soup with duck

Nourishes Yin, warms the stomach and spleen, harmonizes the
intestine, forces Qi, reduces moisture,nourishes blood and liver,
harmonizes liver and spleen, moisturizes, relaxes, builds up Qi,
spreads.
Cooking time approx. 1 1/2 hours
Calories p. portion: 161
6 portions
Allergens: EG

**Quantity of ingredients**
Rice round grain  1 cup /  100g. (yes) ...........................................metal
Water  8 cups /  900g. (yes) ........................................................ earth
Duck (slaughtered)  5/8 lbs - 8oz /  250g. (recommended)........... wood
Shiitake, dried  4-6 pieces /  5g. (yes)........................................... earth
Parsley  2 table spoons /  12g. (recommended)........................... wood
Butter organic  1 teaspoon /  3g. (yes)......................................... earth
Soy sauce  1 dash /  2g. (little) ....................................................water

**Cooking instructions:**
Soak shiitake mushrooms. Prepare rice soup according to the basic
recipe. Add duck meat and shiitake mushrooms for the last 30 minutes.
Add oyster mushrooms, parsley and a little butter at the very end.
Season with soy sauce.

Variant: Add soaked and cooked adzuki beans. They enhance the
diuretic effect.

## 7.20 Rice congee with chicken liver and buckthorn fruit

Warms the stomach and spleen, harmonizes the intestine, forces Qi, reduces moisture, nourishes liver-blood, nourishes and forces liver, forces kidney, forces blood, makes eyes clear.
Cooking time approx. 3 hours
Calories p. portion: 176
3 portions
Allergens: EO

**Quantity of ingredients**
Basic recipe for a rice soup 5 cups /  800g. (recommended)...............*
Chicken liver  1/2 cup /  60g. (recommended).............................. earth
Bocksdorn fruits, goji berry dried  1/2 cup /  60g. (recommended) wood
Soy sauce  1 dash /  3g. (little) ....................................................water

**Cooking instructions:**
Cook basic recipe for rice congee with the chicken liver and wolfberry fruits; Season with soy sauce.

## 7.21 Rice with parsnips

Regulates Qi, dries out, passes downwardly, warms the stomach and spleen, harmonizes the intestine, forces Qi, reduces moisture. moisturizes, relaxes, builds up Qi, spreads. distributes mucus, activates Wei Qi, forces Qi.
Cooking time approx. 45 min
Calories p. portion: 206
3 portions

**Quantity of ingredients**
Rice variety any  1 cup /  120g. (yes)...........................................metal
Water  1 1/2 cups /  200g. (yes)................................................... earth
Salt  1 pinch /  1g. (recommended)...............................................water
Parsnip  3-4 pieces /  450g. (yes) .................................................. fire
Olive oil  1 table spoon /  10g. (little).............................................. earth
Sage  1 teaspoon /  3g. (yes) ........................................................ fire

**Cooking instructions:**
Peel the parsnips and cut into slices. Fry for a short time in oil. Add the rice and fry again for a short time. Add the water and cook it at least 30 min. Sprinkle with fresh chopped sage.

## 7.22 Roasted millet with Celery sticks

Strengthens spleen and kidney, diuretic, brings the liver Qi in motion, cools heat, moisturizes, relaxes, builds up Qi, spreads.
Cooking time approx. 30 min
Calories p. portion: 400
2 portions
Allergens: L

### Quantity of ingredients
Millet  1 cup /  120g. (recommended)........................................... earth
Water  1 1/2 cups /  240g. (yes)................................................... earth
Celery sticks  2 rods /  50g. (yes) ................................................ earth
Herbs various  1 table spoon /  10g. (yes)...........................................*
Water  2 table spoons /  30g. (yes)............................................... earth
Salt  1 pinch /  1g. (recommended)...............................................water
Sage  3-4 leaves /  2g. (yes)........................................................... fire
Cress  1 teaspoon /  3g. (yes).....................................................metal

### Cooking instructions:
Roast millet briefly, pour over water, heat till it boils and let stand for 20 min. to swell.

Cut celery into small pieces and mix with water, salt and fresh herbs and cook for 10 min. Add to the millet. Sprinkle fresh sage or watercress over it.

## 7.23 Roasted nuts

Strengthens kidney Qi, essence and brain, forces kidney, builds up essence, warms lungs, moistens the intestine, moisturizes, relaxes, builds up Qi, spreads.
Cooking time approx. 5 min
Calories p. portion: 973
2 portions
Allergens: H

### Quantity of ingredients
Hazelnuts  1/4 lbs - 4oz /  100g. (recommended)......................... earth
Cashews  1/4 lbs - 4oz /  100g. (yes)............................................ earth
Walnuts  1/4 lbs - 4oz /  100g. (recommended)............................ earth

### Cooking instructions:
Roast nuts in a pan for about 5 minutes.

## 7.24 Spinach with Tahini

Nourishes blood and Yin, forces Zang-organs, forces stomach and intestines, harmonizes Qi, moisturizes lungs, forces Qi, forces spleen, relieves inflammation, moisturizes, relaxes, builds up Qi, spreads, nourishes blood.
Cooking time approx. 20 min
Calories p. portion: 150
4 portions
Allergens: N

**Quantity of ingredients**
Potato  1,1 lbs /  500g. (yes)........................................................ earth
Salt  1 pinch /  0,2g. (recommended)..........................................water
Water  1 cup /  25g. (yes)........................................................... earth
Spinach  2,2 lbs /  800g. (recommended) ................................... earth
Sesame paste (Tahini)  2 table spoons /  20g. (recommended) ... earth

**Cooking instructions:**
Cook potatoes and peel. Heat water. Blanch spinach. Shake off water and let it dry and stir with sesame.

## 7.25 Tea from coriander

Sudorific, reduces wind.
Cooking time approx. 10 min
Calories p. portion: 2
4 portions

**Quantity of ingredients**
Coriander  1 teaspoon /  3g. (recommended)..............................metal
Water  2 cup /  500g. (yes) ......................................................... earth

**Cooking instructions:**
Heat the water till it boils and put it aside. Add coriander and 10 min. to let go. Sweet to taste with honey. Strain when pouring.

## 7.26 Tea from Fructus Lycii

Strengthens blood and fluids, regulates Qi, produces humors, calms the mind, forces Qi.
Cooking time approx. 10 min
Calories p. portion: 3
4 portions

**Quantity of ingredients**
Lychee  2 teaspoons /  18g. (recommended)....................................*
Water  2 cup /  500g. (yes).......................................................... earth

**Cooking instructions:**
Heat the water till it boils and put it aside. Add Fructus Lyecii and keep
for 10 min. to let go. Sweet to taste with honey.

## 7.27  Tea from lemon

Cools heat, preserves the fluids, contracts.
Cooking time approx. 5 min
Calories p. portion: 10
1 portions

**Quantity of ingredients**
Lemon juice  1 table spoon /  10g. (recommended) .................... wood
Water  1 cup /  120g. (yes).......................................................... earth

**Cooking instructions:**
In a cup with hot water add the lemon juice. Drink in small sips.

## 7.28  Tea from licorice (heart-strengthening)

Strengthen spleen and stomach Qi, nourishes Yin from heart and
kidney, moisturizes, forces heart and kidney, reduces internal heat,
preserves the fluids, contracts.
Cooking time approx. 15 min
Calories p. portion: 20
4 portions

**Quantity of ingredients**
Licorice root tea  2-4 teaspoons /  6g. (recommended) ......................*
Dates red  2 table spoons (chopped) /  20g. (recommended)....... earth
Wheat  2 teaspoons (milled) /  16g. (yes).................................... wood
Water  2 cup /  500g. (yes).......................................................... earth

**Cooking instructions:**
Simmer licorice root, red dates and wheat for 40 minutes, strain and
keep the tea in the refrigerator. Throw away the ingredients.
Variant: This recipe can be supplemented with chicken broth; it will be
even stronger. Decoction: 2-4 teaspoons, sprinkle licorice with 1/2 liter
of cold water, heat till it boils, cook for 1 min, leave for 10 min. Drink 1

cup twice a day.

## 7.29 Tea from longane

Forces spleen, builds up lung, builds up heart, calms nerves.
Cooking time approx. 10 min
Calories p. portion: 0
4 portions

**Quantity of ingredients**
Longane  2 teaspoons /  4g. (yes) ........................................................ *
Water  2 cup /  500g. (yes) ........................................................ earth

**Cooking instructions:**
Heat the water till it boils and put it aside. Add Longane and 10 min. to
let go. Sweet to taste with honey. Strain when pouring.

## 7.30 Tea from rose hip

Strengthens spleen Qi.
Cooking time approx. 10 min
Calories p. portion: 2
4 portions

**Quantity of ingredients**
Rose hip tea  2 table spoons /  4g. (little) .................................... wood
Water  2 cup /  500g. (yes) ........................................................ earth

**Cooking instructions:**
Heat the water till it boils and put it aside. Add rosehip and leave for 10
min. to let go. Sweet to taste with honey. Strain when pouring.

## 7.31 Tea from rosemary

Dries out, passes downwardly, forces heart, lung and spleen Qi, forces
liver-blood, forces heart-Yin, expels spleen heat / cold moisture,
strengthens spleen and kidney Yang.
Cooking time approx. 15 min
Calories p. portion: 1
4 portions

**Quantity of ingredients**
Rosemary  2-4 teaspoons /  6g. (little) ............................................ fire
Water  2 cup /  500g. (yes) ........................................................ earth

**Cooking instructions:**
Heat the water till it boils and put it aside. Add rosemary and 10 min. to let go. Strain. Sweet to taste with honey.

## 7.32 Tsampa with jam or fruit compote

Nourishes fluids, reduces stomach heat, forces spleen, produces essence, harmonizes stomach, moisturizes intestines.
Cooking time approx. 5 min
Calories p. portion: 280
1 portions
Allergens: AGO

**Quantity of ingredients**
Tsampa (roasted barley flour)  2 table spoons /  30g. (rec.) ......... earth
Water  6-8 table spoons /  70g. (yes)........................................... earth
Butter organic  1/2 teaspoon /  2g. (yes)...................................... earth
Strawberry jam  1 table spoon /  7g. (recommended)................... wood
Sunflower seeds  2 teaspoons /  14g. (recommended) ................ earth
Apple (sweet)  1 piece grated /  120g. (yes)................................ earth

**Cooking instructions:**
Pour tsampa with boiling water and stir with a spoon until a porridge is formed.
Add butter, jam, sunflower seeds and grated apple.
Sweet to taste with honey, whole cane sugar, or barley malt.
Spices and herbs: fresh mint, vanilla or cocoa, anise, cinnamon

Summer: jam or compote of your choice
Winter: nuts and apple or pear

# 8 Effects of food

## 8.1 Use ingredients: recommendable

Acai powder
Acerola fruit nectar or powder
Agave nectar
Agrimony
Almond
Amaranth Pops
Angelica root
Apple puree
Apricot dried
Apricot jam
Apricot nectar
Apricots juice
Baking powder
Banchatee (green tea)
barberry
Barley
Barley flour
Barley grass powder
Barley grouts
Barley malt
Barley not peeled
Basic recipe for a beef soup
Basic recipe for a beef soup (warming)
Basic recipe for a chicken soup
(warming)
Basic recipe for a duck soup
Basic recipe for a fish soup
Basic recipe for a rice soup (Congee)
Basic recipe for a vegetable soup
(nutritious)
Bay leaf
Beans (green, fresh)
Bearberry leaf
Beef bone marrow
Beef heart
Beef heart (calf)
Beef kidney
Beef liver
Beef lungs (calf)
Beef Oxtail pieces
Beef soup meat
Beef stomach
Beer (alcohol-free)
Beer (alcohol-reduced)
Berries of the season
Berry juice
Bitter Herb liqueur
Bitter Lemon
Bitter liqueur

Bitter orange peel
Black beans
Black fungus mushroom
Blackberry dried (unripe fruit)
Blackberry jam
Blackberry leaves
Blackberry´s
Blackthorn (Sloe)
Blue mallow tee
Blueberry
Blueberry dried
Blueberry jam
Blueberry juice
Bocksdorn fruits (Fructus Lycii, Goji,
goji berry dried
Borage
Brazil nuts
Bread roll
Bread with carob kernel flour
Breadcrumbs (wheat bread, bread roll)
Brie cheese
Brown ale
Buckbean
Buckwheat (roasted) Kasha
Buckwheat whole grain
Bush beans
Butter (half fat)
Butter beans white
Calamari
Camembert
Campari
Capers in olive oil
Cardamom
Carob flour, St. john's bread
Chamomile
Chamomile tea
Channa-Dal
Chard
Chenpi (chinese tangerine bowl)
Cherry
Cherry (sour)
Cherry compote
Chervil
Chervil dried
Chestnut puree
Chicken Blood
Chicken egg white
Chicken heart
Chicken liver

Chicken meat
Chicken stomach
Chicken yolk
Chickweed
Chicory
Chinese pearl barley
Chlorella (fresh water)
Chocolate
Chocolate (Diabetic)
Chrysanthemum blossom tea
Clarified butter
Clementine
Coconut fat
Coconut meat
Codfish
Cola drink
Cola drink (low calorie)
Compote (fruits of the season)
Coriander
Coriander (fresh)
Corn (roasted)
Corn flour
Corn germ oil
Corn silk tea
Corn starch
Cottage cheese
Cranberries
Cranberry
Cranberry jam
Cream (30% fat)
Cream 10% coffee cream
Cream sour 10%
Cream sour 20%
Cream sour 30%
Creamer
Créme fraiche cheese
Crispbread
Cucumber (bitter)
Cucumber (spicy cucumber)
Currant jam (black)
Currant jam (red)
Currant juice (black)
Currants (black)
Currants (red)
Daisy
Dandelion juice
Dashi
Dates red
Deer's Bones
Deer's kidneys
Duck (heart)
Duck (slaughtered)
Ducks egg
Dulse (seaweed)

Dyer's broom herb
Edam cheese
Eel
Eel smoked
Elderberries
Elderberry blossom tee
Emmental cheese
Fennel seeds ground
Fenugreek (Trigonella foenum-graecum)
Fernet Branca (herbal bitter liqueur)
Feta cheese
Fish innards
Fish remains
Fish sauce
Flounder
Flower pollen
Fox nut, gorgon nut, makhana
Fresh cheese from soya
Fresh cheese with herbs
Freshwater crab
Freshwater fish
Fructose (glucose)
Fruit mix juice
Fruit tea
Gail plum
Galangal
Garam Masala powder
Gelatin white
Gelee Royal
Gentian root
Ginkgo fruit
Ginseng
Ginseng liqueur
Ginseng root
Goat and sheep's blood
Goat and sheep's brain
Goat and sheep's liver
Goat and sheep's stomach
Goose blood
Goose fat
Gorgonzola
Gouda cheese
Grape juice red
Grapefruit dried peel
Grapes red
Grapeseed oil
Grass carp
Greengage
Guava
Halibut (Flatfish)
Hazelnuts
Herbal tea mix
Herbs bitter

Herbs of Provence
Hibiscus
Hibiscus tea
Hijiki
Hokkaido pumpkin
Honey wine (Met)
Hop
Horehound leaves
Horse meat
Jasmine blossoms tee
Jellyfish
Kaki plum
Kalmus
Kidney beans (red)
King Solomon's-seal
Kudzu
Kukicha tea
Ladyfingers
Lamb liver
Lavender blossoms
Leaf salads (bitter)
Lemon
Lemon Balm (dried)
Lemon Balm (fresh)
Lemon juice
Lemon peel
Lemongrass
Licorice root tea
Lily bulbs
Lima beans
Lime blossom tea
Linseed
Linseed (crushed)
Liver smoothing tea
Loquate / Japanese medlar
Lotus roots
Lotus seeds
Lovage seeds
Luo Han Guo fruit
Lychee
Lychee in Preserved
Lychee liqueur
Lye roll
Mango juice
Manioc flour
Mare's milk
Martini
Mascarpone cheese
Mayonnaise 50%
Mayonnaise 80%
Mediterranean fish (cod, plaice, haddock, sea eel, mackerel)
Medlar
Millet

Millet flakes
Mineral water
Mirabelle plum
Miso black (fermented)
Mixed Pickles
Mu Erh Mushroom
Muesli
Mulled Wine Spice
Multi-grain bread (gray bread)
Mustard
Mustard Dijon
Mustard medium hot
Mustard sweet
Nasturtium (nose-twister or nose-tweaker)
Nectarine
Nettles
Noodles (wheat) with egg
Noodles (wheat, lasagne) with egg
Noodles (wheat, ribbon noodles) with egg
Noodles (wheat, spaghetti) with egg
Noodles (whole grain) with egg
Nori, purple seaweed, red algae
Octopus
Octopus
Olives green
Orange blossom
Orange dried peel
Orange grated peel
Orange jam
Orange peel
Oregano fresh
Oyster shell powder
Palm oil
Parsley
Parsley root
Passion blossoms tea
Passion fruit
Peanut (roasted)
Peanut butter
Pearl barley
Pearl barley
Pepper powder (hot)
Peppermint
Peppermint tea
Pepperoni
Pepperoni, red, pitted, halved
Pepperoni, yellow, pitted, halved
Peppers (sweet)
Peppers powder
Perch
Pickle
Pig blood

Pigeon egg
Pinto beans speckled
Plum dried
Plums
Pork Bacon
Pork brain
Pork fat (lard)
Pork ham
Pork ham cooked
Pork ham smoked
Pork heart
Pork kidneys
Pork Lard
Pork lung
Pork marrow bones
Pork sausage (Bratwurst) Pork skin
Pork stomach
Pork/beef sausage (smoked)
Pork's intestine
Potato (mealy)
Potato flour
Prickly pear
Processed cheese 12%
processed cheese 30%
Prosecco
Psyllium seed
Pudding powder vanilla
Puff pastry
Pumpernickel (dark bread)
Quinoa
Rabbit (wild)
Rabbit liver
Radicchio
Radish horseradish
Radish leaves
Raspberry
Raspberry jam
Raspberry leaf tea
Red beet
Red berry (without sugar)
Red wine
Ribworttea
Rice (Gaoliang / Sorghum)
Rice long grain rice
Rice mash
Rice starch
Rice sticky
Rice sweet
Rose blossom tea
Rose leaf tea
Rum
Rusk
Rye wholemeal bread
Safflower (Dyer's thistle / Hong Hua)

Sake
Salt
Salt (herbal)
Savory
Savoy cabbage / kale
Sea buckthorn
Sea cucumber
Sesame oil roasted
Sesame paste (Tahini)
Sesame, black
Sesame, white
Sheep's milk yoghurt
Sherry (whine)
Skim milk powder
Slug
Sourdough
Soy flour
Soy noodles
Soy Tofu smoked
Soya Cuisine (soy cream)
Soybeans
Soybeans, blacks, fermented
Spelled flakes
Spinach
Spurdog (spiny dogfish, Schillerlocken)
St. Benedict's thistle, blessed thistle,
holy thistle, spotted thistle
Stevia (candyleaf, sweetleaf)
Strawberry jam
Sugar - icing sugar
Sugar palm sugar
Sugar substitute (sweetener)
Sunflower seeds
Supplementary nutrition
Tabasco
Tea mixture uric acid lowering
Thyme dried
Toast bread (whole grain)
Tomato dried
Tomato juice
Tomato paste
Tomato puree
Tonic Water
Trout (smoked)
Truffle
Tsampa (roasted barley flour)
Tuna
Turkey breast meat
Turkey ham
Turmeric (yellow root)
Turnip
Turnips
Umeboshi paste
Valerian

Vanilla pod
Vanilla sugar natural
Vinegar (Red wine vinegar)
Vinegar Aceto Balsamico
Vinegar Aceto Balsamico white
Walnuts
Walnuts roasted
Water hot
Wax gourd
Wheat flatbread/pita bread
Wheat flour whole grain
Wheat/Rye/Gray-black bread with yeast
Wheatgrass juice
Wheatgrass powder
Whey
White bread (baguette)
White bread (pretzel sticks)
White bread (roll)

White bread (wheat bread)
White breadcrumbs
White cabbage
White dumpling bread (wheat bread cut into chunks)
Whitefish
Whole grain bread
Wholemeal flour
Wild garlic (garlic spinach)
Wild herbs
Wild strawberries
Wormwood
Wormwood herb
Yam root, yam root tuber
Yarrow
Yeast
Yew nut
Yoghurt vanilla

## 8.2  Use ingredients: yes

Adzuki beans
Almond marzipan
Almond milk
Almond puree
Apple (sweet)
Apple juice (natural cloudy)
Apricot
Apricots
Arrowroot
Artichoke
Aubergine
Banana
Banana (cooking banana)
Beef fillet
Beef meat
Beef meat (calf)
Beef meatbones
Boletus mushroom
Borage oil
Broad beans (thick beans)
Broccoli
Buckwheat
Butter organic
Carp
Carrot
Carrot (Early Carrot)
Carrot juice without sugar
Cashews
Cauliflower
Celery root
Celery sticks
Champignon
Chanterelle

Chestnuts
Chickpeas
Chinese cabbage
Coconut flakes
Coconut grated
Coconut milk
Coix (seeds) YiYi Ren
Corn
Corn (fast polenta)
Corn Grease (Polenta)
Cow's milk (1.5% fat)
Cow's milk (whole milk 3.5% fat)
Cress
Dates dried
Evening primrose oil
Fennel
Fig
Fig dried
Fish pieces mixed (fresh water)
French beans
Goose
Goose egg
Goose parts
Gourd
Grape juice white
Grapes white
Herbs various
Herbs wild
Lentils black
Lentils red
Linseed oil
Longane
Malt

Maple syrup
Miso
Morel (black, dried)
Morel, dried
Mozzarella
Mung bean
Okra
Olives
Oyster mushroom
Oysters
Parmesan
Parsnip
Peanuts
Pear
Peas
Peas, green
Peppers
Pigeon
Pine nuts
Pistachios
Pork knuckle
Pork liver
Pork meat
Potato
Pumpkin
Pumpkin seeds
Quail
Quail egg
Quince
Rabbit
Radish
Radish black
Raisins
Red cabbage
Reishi mushroom
Rice (fragrance)
Rice (whole grain)
Rice Basmati

Rice black
Rice flour
Rice malt
Rice noodles
Rice red
Rice round grain
Rice variety any
Rice wild (nature rice)
Rye
Rye flour
Saffron
Sage
Sago (cereals)
Salsify
Sesame oil
Shiitake, dried
Soy Tofu
Soybean milk
Soybeans, black
Soybeans, yellow
Sugar molasses
Sweet potato
Topinambur
Trout
Vanilla
Vanilla powder
Vegetable juice
Water
Wheat
Wheat bran
Wheat bulgur
Wheat flakes
Wheat flour
Wheat semolina
Wheat semolina for children
White beans
White wine
Zucchini

## 8.3   Use ingredients: little

Agar agar (kelp)
Aloe juice
Anise (Common Fennel)
Apple (sour)
Balm
Batavia
Bean oil
Beer (Pils)
Beer (Top-fermented German dark beer)
Black caraway
Black-eyed peas

Bulgur (cereals)
Buttermilk
Caviar
Cherry juice
Chicken egg
Chives
Clementines
Clove
Cooking oil
Couscous
Cranberry
Cranberry juice

Cream, sweet 30%
Cumin (Caraway seed)
Curd cheese 20%
Curd cheese 40%
Currant (black)
Currant (red)
Currant (white)
Deer meat
Deer meat
Dill
Endive salad
Fennel tea
Fresh cheese
Ginger fresh
Ginger oil
Gooseberry
Green spelt
Ground
Ground caraway
Hawthorn
Iceberg lettuce
Kefir
Kohlrabi
Kombu seaweed (Saccharina japonica)
Kumquats
Lamb's lettuce
Lamb's lettuce
Leek
Lentils
Lentils yellow
Lettuce
Lobster
Mallow (Malva sylvestris) blossom tea
Margarine
Margarine (diet)
Marjoram
Miso paste (soy bean paste)
Mustard seeds
Nutmeg
Oat
Oat flakes (whole grain)
Oat flakes roasted
Oat flour
Oat fusion (baby food)
Oat meal
Oat milk
Olive oil
Onion (shallot)

Onion (spring onion)
Onion read
Onion white
Orange
Oregano dried
Peaches
Peaches (canned)
Peanut oil
Pear juice
Pheasant
Pomegranate
Pumpkin seed oil
Rabbit meat
Rapeseed oil
Raspberry dried (immature)
Romaine lettuce / lettuce salad
Rose hip
Rose hip tea
Rosemary
Sauerkraut (cutted cabbage fermented)
Shrimp
Shrimps
Sour cherries
Sour cream 15% fat
Sour milk
Sour milk cheese 20%
Soy sauce
Soybean oil
Spelled (Dark) bread
Spelled grain
Spelled semolina
Spelled wholemeal flour
Spiny lobsters
Star anise
Strawberries
Strawberry Juice
Sugar brown
Sunflower oil
Tangerine
Tarragon (Estragon)
Thistle oil
Thyme
Umeboshi plums (Japanese apricots)
Vinegar (Apple vinegar)
Wakame
Walnut oil
Wheat germ oil
Wild boar meat

## 8.4 Do not use contra-acting foods

Amaranth
Anchovy / Sardine
Asparagus (green or white)

Avocado
Bamboo shoots
Basil

Basil (fresh)
Black tea
Boxhorn clover seeds
Brussels sprouts
Burdock root tea
Cantaloupe
Carambola (Star fruit)
Cereal coffee
Chili (pod or ground)
Cinnamon ground
Cinnamon sticks
Cocoa
Cod
Coffee
Crab
Crucian
Cucumber
Curcuma
Curry
Curry paste red
Dandelion (young plants)
Dandelionroots tea
Feta cheese
Garlic
Gentian root tea
Ginger powder
Goat
Goat and sheep's milk
Goat cheese
Grapefruit (Pomelo)
Grapefruit juice
Green tea
Herring
Honey
Hyssop
Juniper berry
Kiwi
Lamb bones
Lamb kidneys
Lamb meat
Lamb shoulder
Lime
Lovage
Mackerel
Mango

Mold cheese
Mulberry fruit
Mullet
Mung bean sprouting
Mussels
Mutton
Mutton
Orange juice
Papaya
Pepper (ground)
Pepper Cayenne
Pepper white (ground)
Peppercorns
Peppers (rose peppers)
Pimento
Pineapple
Pineapple (from a can)
Pineapple juice without sugar
Plaice
Plum
Poppy
Radish (white, green, purple-red)
Rhubarb
Rosefish
Rucola
Salmon
Seacrab
Shark
Sheep's milk
Sorrel
Spirit
Sugar candy white
Sugar cane sugar
Sugar fructose - fruit sugar
Sugar glucose - grapes sugar
Sugar Milk Sugar
Sugar white
Tomato
Watermelon
Wheat beer
Yarrow tea
Yogi tea
Yogurt (natural, 1.5% fat)
Yogurt (natural, 3.5% fat)

# 9 Herbs and their effects

## 9.1 Basil

thermal effect: warm
taste: spicy, bitter
Dries out, leads down. Tonifies Yang and Qi, dissolves mucus-cold, eliminates wind-cold.
It has a beneficial effect on flatulence and nausea, relaxing and soothing.
Good to fight emphysema, bronchitis, whooping cough, high blood pressure, headache, mouth odor, warts, hiccup, gout, migraine.

## 9.2 Coriander

thermal effect: warm
taste: spicy
Driving sweat, reducing wind, draining moisture, tonifying and regulating qi, eliminating wind-cold. The essential oils are appetizing, digestive, cramping and soothing in stomach and intestinal disorders.

## 9.3 Herbs various

Stimulates appetite. Effect different.
Appetizing, lots of trace elements and vitamins.

## 9.4 Cress

thermal effect: cool
taste: sweet
Moves and tonifies qi and blood, diuretic, cools in internal heat, moisturizes lungs, triggers stagnation, heads upwards.
Diuretic, supports urination. Good to fight dry mouth, inner agitation, sore throat, diabetes, kidney stones, gastrointestinal complaints, lung problems, menstrual cramps or cancer.

## 9.5 Lily bulbs

thermal effect: cool
taste: sweet, bitter
Tonifies Yin, soothes Shen / Spirit. Moisturizes the lungs, clears heat and stops coughing.
Calms nerves, good to fight  scaly skin. The onions and the petals are added to ointments in the Orient, which can heal muscles and tendons.
White lily (astringent).

## 9.6 Marjoram

thermal effect: warm
taste: spicy
Dissolves stagnation, heads upwards. Regulates and moves Qi, eliminates wind-cold, dissolves slime-cold, calms down Shen / Spirit, suppresses inner wind, moves blood.
Helps to digest fat foods, strengthens digestive organs, helps to fight colds, strengthens menstruation, promotes skin healing.

## 9.7 Parsley

thermal effect: warm
taste: bitter
Nourishes blood and liver, harmonizes liver and spleen, strengthens eyesight, preserves juices, contracts. Dissolves moisture and warms Yang.
Stimulates liver function, detoxifies. Forces urinating. Relieves flatulence. Digestive and menstrual stimulating, birth-accelerating, memory-enhancing, blood-purifying, skin-smoothing.

## 9.8 Rosemary

thermal effect: warm
taste: bitter
Dries out, leads down. Strengthens the heart, lungs and spleen qi, strengthens liver blood. Strengthens heart-Yin. Expels spleen heat / cold moisture. Strengthens spleen and kidney yang.
Promotes digestion, relieves bloating, strengthens lung, spleen and kidney. Affects the circulation and nerves. Appetizing. Baths help to fight circulatory disorders as well as with gout and rheumatism.

## 9.9 Sage

thermal effect: neutral
taste: bitter, spicy
Expels slime, guides down, strengthens Qi, eliminates Wind-Heat, eliminate heat induced by Yin deficiency.
Good to fight yeast infections. The leaves have a digestive effect and are used in greasy foods. Antiperspirant effect. Helps to relieve coughing attacks. Dries out.

## 9.10 King Solomon's-seal

thermal effect: neutral
taste: sweet, bitter
Tonifies Yin and Qi, astringent, tonifies blood, eliminates wind-cold / heat-wetness.
Used to repair wounds or damaged tissue. Good to fight dry cough, earlier also tuberculosis and dysentery, as well as diarrhea and hemorrhoids.

## 9.11 Yam root, yam root tuber

thermal effect: neutral
taste: sweet
Tonifies Yin, Yang and Qi, reduces inner wind, dissolves wetness, warms Yang.
Solves cramps (in the gastrointestinal tract). Digestive through increased bile production. Anti-inflammatory in rheumatic diseases.
Mucolytic agent for coughing. Relief of menopausal symptoms.

## 9.12 Lemon Balm (fresh)

thermal effect: cool
taste: sour
Soothes Shen / Spirit, regulates and moves Qi, eliminates heat caused by Yin deficiency, tones Qi.
Stimulating, antibacterial, encouraging, relaxing, antispasmodic, cooling, antipyretic, analgesic, sweat-inducing, virus-
inhibiting. Good for colds, fever, flu, cough, bronchitis, asthma, loss of appetite, bloating, heartburn.

# 10 Basics of Nutrition

The basic principles of nutrition described herein are general recommendations. They are not aimed at a specific form of therapy. Recommendations concerning a therapy have priority.

## 10.1 Nutrition

Regular meals in a relaxed atmosphere. A warm breakfast is considered a good start into the day.
The main meals ought to be taken for lunch – supper in the early evening. Pay attention to feeling hungry or sated: don't eat too much nor remain hungry is the rule
Prepare the meals freshly from natural, regional products. Frozen, heat-conserved, industrially prepared or foodstuffs cooked in the microwave oven are rejected.
Choice of foodstuffs according to the season: more cooling food in summer, more warming food in winter.
Eat cooked food at least twice a day. Food and drinks ought to be lukewarm, never ice-cold or hot.
Raw vegetables, briefly cooked vegetables, freshly squeezed juices and mineral water are not recommended. Milk and dairy products are only included in the diet if they don't cause problems. Don't use therapeutic recipes over a longer period without consulting your doctor or therapist.

**Varied food**
Enjoy the diversity of foodstuffs. Characteristics of a balanced nutrition are variety, suitable combination and a balanced quantity of rich and low energy foodstuffs (on one hand avoiding undersupply with essential nutrients and on the other hand to take to many undesirable substances).

**A lot of Cereal Products - and Potatoes**
Bread, pasta, rice, cereal flakes (best wholemeal) as well as potatoes contain almost no fat, but many vitamins, mineral nutrients, trace elements, roughage and secondary plant substances. These foodstuffs ought to be taken with low-fat side dishes.

**Vegetables and Fruit – „Take Five" every day ...** 5 portions of vegetables and fruit a day, as fresh as possible, briefly cooked, or maybe one portion as a juice – ideal as a side dish to every meal as well as snack between meals: Thus a lot of vitamins, mineral nutrients as well as roughage and secondary plant substances

### Daily milk and dairy products
Milk and Dairy Products every Day, once or twice per Week Fish; meat, sausages as well as eggs moderately. These foodstuffs contain valuable nutrients like calcium in the milk, iodine selenium and omega-3 fat acids in saltwater fish. Meat is favorable due to its high content of disposable iron and the vitamins B1, B6 and B12. Quantities of 300 – 600 g meat and sausage per week are sufficient. Prefer low-fat products, especially in meat- and dairy products.

### Low-fat and fatty Foodstuffs
Fat supplies us with essential fat acids and fatty foodstuffs contain also fat-soluble vitamins. Fat is high in energy; therefore much fat in the food may cause overweight, possibly also cancer. Too many saturated fat acids may further a tendency for cardio-vascular diseases in the long term. Prefer vegetable oils and fats (e.g. rapeseed-, olive-, soya-oils and solid fats produced therefrom). Beware of invisible fat in meat- and dairy products, pastry and sweets as well as in fast-food and convenience foods. 70 – 90 g fat per day is sufficient.

### Moderately Sugar and Salt
Take sugar and foods/drinks containing various kinds of sugar (e.g. glucose syrup) only occasionally. Use herbs and spices as well as a little salt creatively. Prefer salt containing iodine.

### Plenty of Liquids
Water is absolutely essential. Drink 1-2 l liquids every day. Prefer water (with or without gas) and other low-calorie drinks. Alcoholic drinks should not be taken.

### Tasty Dishes, carefully cooked
Cook the meals with as low temperatures and as short as possible, using little water and fat – this preserves the original taste, keeps the nutrients intact and prevents the production of harmful compounds.

### Take time and enjoy the food
Take your Time and enjoy your Food
Eating consciously helps to eat right. The eye enjoys food, too. It's fun, invites to enjoy varied dishes and stimulates the feeling of satiety.

### Watch your Weight and stay in Motion
A balanced diet and a lot of exercise and sport (30 – 60 min/day) are a healthy combination. The right weight furthers well-being and health. Thermals, directional effectiveness, digestive power

There are various criteria for judging the effectiveness of herbs and foodstuffs.

The use of certain herbs and ingredients is based on observations of the effects on the body which these foodstuffs, herbs and spices show after having eaten them. The medical science has developed following system: Every ingredient or herb has a directional effectiveness. Furthermore, there are herbs which have a special effect on certain organs.

The basic condition for a healthy metabolism is to obtain sufficient energy from food and that the digestive process doesn't use too much energy. An easily digestible meal makes content and sated, doesn't cause flatulence and fatigue after the meal. The perfect spices increase the healthiness of our meals. Very often, just small doses of herbs and spices will suffice. They are not used to make us sated, but to help our digestive organs to digest the food.

## 10.2 Recipes

The recipes list the ingredients to be used and the cooking instructions show how the dish is prepared. The list of ingredients shows the concerned quantities as well as the relevance for the therapy. If you find „less than mentioned", try to comply or find an alternative from the „list of recommended foodstuffs". Mostly it shall result just in a small change of taste when you simply avoid this ingredient.

Mild cooking methods: boiling, stewing, poaching, steaming
Strong cooking methods: barbecuing, roasting, frying, smoking
Balanced cooking methods: deep-frying, baking brick
Deep-freezing and warming in the microwave oven should be avoided (denaturalization).

## 10.3 Foodstuffs

Foodstuffs have an effect on body and soul like medicinal herbs, only a very much milder one. Dietary advice is mainly based on regional foodstuffs. The knowledge about the effects of each foodstuff and the knowledge, when which foodstuff shall be used, is based on the orthodox school of medicine. Use ecologic-organic products, if possible. As everything should be cooked for a long time due to a better digestability and very rarely eaten raw, the food agrees with everyone.

The classification of the foodstuffs according to their effect on the body is the basis in order to achieve a harmonious status of health.

Dietary advisors do not recommend certain foodstuffs for everyone. The individual diet is tailor-made for the individual constitution.

Buy only fresh and ripe fruit and vegetables. You ought to leave unripe fruit and vegetables and such with brown spots and wilted leaves behind in the market. In this case take deep-frozen goods (never ready-to-serve dishes!). Fruit and vegetables are deep-frozen immediately after harvesting and often contain more vitamins and minerals than the goods from the vegetable shelf. Whereas conserved or tinned goods contain very much less biological substances. Also, salt, sugar and others are mostly added to the latter. Never leave the foodstuffs in the water after washing them to avoid that many vital substances get drowned. Clean salads, fruit and vegetables immediately before serving.

Please make sure of the hygienic processing of foodstuffs. Clean your salads, fruit and vegetables carefully. When cooking with meat, prepare all ingredients first and then process the meat products. Clean the worktop and tools very carefully. Wooden surfaces ought to be treated with a mild disinfectant regularly in order to reduce germination.
Store fruit and vegetables separately, if possible. Harvested fruit and vegetables are still alive and emit e.g. ethylene gas, which makes other products ripen and age faster. Keep meat and fish in the closed packaging or store them in the fridge in closed containers.

## 10.4 Herbs

There are some basic rules for storing medicinal herbs. On principle, herbs must be protected from direct sunlight, humidity and heat.

Containers for the storage of herbs may be glasses, ceramic jars and even plastic containers. However, plastic is a rather unsuitable material and should only be a short-term solution. In case of glass containers, use a dark material.

Medicinal herbs cannot be kept for any long period. The shelf life of herbs is limited. However, it can be prolonged with suitable storage. The place should be dark, rather cool and absolutely dry. A wooden medicine cabinet, placed not directly next to a source of heat, would be ideal. Never buy large quantities of herbs so as not to have to throw them away. Label the container with the name of the herb and the date of harvesting or processing.

# 11 Other dietic-books

The following syndromes of dietetics, TCM or for a therapy supplement for cancer are available.

## Dietetics

E001. Nutrition of the infant - baby food
E002. Nutrition during lactation
E003. Nutrition in old age
E004. Nutrition of children and adolescents
E005. Nutrition of athletes
E006. Light weight
E007. Pregnancy
E008. Full food

**Protein and electrolyte - kidneys**
E009. (hemodialysis) dialysis treatment
E010. Acute renal failure
E011. Chronic renal insufficiency
E012. Nephrotic syndrome
E013. Kidney stones (nephrolithiasis)

**Gastrointestinal tract - pancreas**
E014. Acute pancreatitis (inflammation of the pancreas)
E015. Chronic pancreatitis (inflammation of the pancreas)

**Gastrointestinal tract - small intestine and large intestine**
E016. Acute obstipation (constipation)
E017. Chronic obstipation (constipation)
E018. Colon irritabile
E019. Diverticulitis
E020. Acquired lactose intolerance (lactose malabsorption)
E021. Fructose malabsorption
E022. Glutensensitive enteropathy (celiac disease)
E023. Colectomy
E024. Short Bowel Syndrome

**Gastrointestinal tract - liver, gallbladder, bile ducts**
E025. Acute and chronic hepatitis (inflammation of the liver)
E026. Cholelithiasis (bile stones)
E027. fatty liver
E028. cirrhosis

**Gastrointestinal tract - Stomach and duodenal intestine**
E029. Acute gastritis
E030. Chronic gastritis
E031. Stomach bleeding
E032. Ulcus ventriculi and duodenal ulcer
E033. Condition after gastric surgery

**Gastrointestinal tract - oral cavity and esophagus**
E034. Stomatitis
E035. Esophageal carcinoma (esophageal cancer)
E036. Refluosophagitis (heartburn)

**Special diseases**
E037. Phenylketonuria (PKU)
E038. Rheumatic joint diseases

E039. **Metabolism** Obesity (overweight)
E040. Diabetes mellitus
E041. Eating disorders (underweight)

**Fat metabolism**
E042. Hypercholesterolaemia (increased cholesterol level)
E043. Hepatic Encephalopathy

**Heart and circulation**
E044. Arteriosclerosis (arterial calcification)
E045. Heart insufficiency
E046. Hypertension
E047. Hyperuricaemia and gout

E048. **Changed nutrient requirements** In case of fever
E049. For malignant diseases
E050. After burns
E051. Radiation and chemotherapy

E100. **CANCER** Pancreatic cancer
E101. Bladder cancer
E102. Blood cancer (leukemia)
E103. Breast cancer
E104. Colorectal cancer
E105. Gastric cancer
E106. Kidney cancer
E107. Esophageal cancer

# TCM
E200. Bladder - moisture heat in the bladder
E201. Bladder - moisture and cold in the bladder
E202. Bladder - emptiness and cold in the bladder
E203. Large intestine - external cold affects the large intestine
E204. Large intestine - moisture heat in the large intestine
E205. Large intestine - heat blocks the intestine II acute
E206. Large intestine - dryness of the colon
E207. Large intestine - Yang deficiency (cold)
E208. Heart - Blood insufficiency
E209. Heart - Blood stagnation
E210. Heart - Fire
E211. Heart - Hot mucus clogs the heart pores
E212. Heart - Cold mucus clogs the heart pores
E213. Heart - Qi deficiency
E214. Heart - Yang deficiency

E215. Heart - Yin deficiency
E216. Liver - Ascending Liver Yang
E217. Liver - Blood deficiency
E218. Liver - Blood stagnation
E219. Liver - Moisture heat in liver and gall bladder
E220. Liver - Fire
E221. Liver - Gall bladder Qi-Empty
E222. Liver - Cold in the liver meridian
E223. Liver - Qi stagnation
E224. Liver - Wind
E225. Liver - Wind with ascending liver Yang
E226. Liver - Wind with blood anemic
E227. Liver - Wind with extreme heat
E228. Lung - Qi deficiency
E229. Lung - Mucus-moisture in the lungs
E230. Lung - Mucus-heat in the lungs
E231. Lung - Mucus-cold in the lungs
E232. Lung - Dryness of the lungs
E233. Lung - Wind-heat attacks the lungs
E234. Lung - Wind-cold affects the lungs
E235. Lung - Yin deficiency
E236. Stomach - Bloodstagnation
E237. Stomach - Fire
E238. Stomach - Cold with liquid
E239. Stomach - Nutrition stagnation
E240. Stomach - Qi deficiency
E241. Stomach - Rebellious Qi
E242. Stomach - Yin Emptiness
E243. Spleen - Heat and moisture attack the spleen
E244. Spleen - Coldness and moisture affects the spleen
E245. Spleen - Qi deficiency
E246. Spleen - Qi deficiency + Declining spleen Qi
E247. Spleen - Qi deficiency + spleen does not control the blood
E248. Spleen - Yang deficiency
E249. Kidney - Heart and kidney no longer communicate
E250. Kidney - Jing deficiency
E251. Kidney - Kidneys cannot receive the Qi
E252. Kidney - Qi is not stable
E253. Kidney - Yang deficiency
E254. Kidney - Yin deficiency


For further information visit di-book.com.